Gender
Issues

Kaye Stearman
& Nikki van der Gaag

Wayland

Global Issues series
Closing the Borders
Crime and Punishment
The Exploitation of Children
Gender Issues
Genetic Engineering
Racism
The Rich–Poor Divide
Terrorism
United Nations – Peacekeeper?
Violence in Society

Book Editors: Serpentine Editorial
Series Editor: Rosemary Ashley
Designer: Simon Borrough

First published in 1995 by Wayland (Publishers) Ltd
61 Western Road, Hove, East Sussex BN3 1JD, England

© Copyright 1995 Wayland (Publishers) Ltd

British Library Cataloguing in Publication Data
Stearman, Kaye
Gender Issues. – (Global Issues Series)
I. Title II. Gaag, Nikki van der
III. Series
305.3
ISBN 0 7502 1515 1

Typeset by Simon Borrough
Printed and bound by G. Canale C.S.p.a., Turin, Italy

Cover picture: In Western countries young people enjoy mixed company at work and at leisure.

Title page picture: These were the first women to work for a company in Kuwait, in the Middle East.

The authors would like to thank Tina Wallace, Lynne Gerlach,
Rachel Warner and Ling Fang Cheng
for their help with this book.

Picture acknowledgements
Camera Press 6,18,39,41,42,43; Chapel Studios 57; Greg Evans cover, /P. Ferraby 33; Eye Ubiquitous /D. Cumming 24(above), /M. Alkins 28, 29, /T. Benjamin 47, /J. Waterlow 54, /M. McKee 59; Impact /C. Cormack 10, /S. Benbow 11 (below), /P. Menzel 12-13, /P. Cavendish 15, /M. Henley 16, /R. Morton 20, /A le Garsmeur 16, /C. Penn 22 & 23, /P. Arkell 25,& 28, /P. Cavendish 26-7,/ P.Sellers 34 /C. Bluntzer 35, /A. Mason 44; Panos 30, /P. Tweedie 40 & title page & 50-51, 55; Rowe 7, 11(above); Tony Stone Worldwide /P. Correz 4-5, /B. Torrez 32, /G. Brad Lewis 51; Topham Picture Source 8, 36, 37, 49, 50, 56; Trip /J & F. Teede 9, /H. Rogers 14, /J. Wakelin contents & 17, /V. Shuba 48. The cartoon on page 11 is reproduced by kind permission of the copyright holder © Viv Quillin

CONTENTS

Women in African countries may tend crops and animals, and bring up children on their own, while their husbands work in cities far away.

UNDERSTANDING GENDER

'He's a real little boy, isn't he? Always fighting.'

'Isn't she a pretty little girl?'

'Typical woman, just won't make up her mind!'

'When it comes to practical things, give me a man every time.'

Our ideas about gender roles are formed early in life but they may change as we grow into adults.

What is it that makes every person either female or male? We rarely ask this question, mostly we just accept that everyone falls into one category or the other. The answer is very complex. Part of it is concerned with our bodies, especially the microscopic information-carriers called chromosomes, and substances called hormones.

Our bodies are only a starting point. As we grow older, what we are (our personality) is influenced more and

more by the world around us (our society). We use the word 'gender' to cover the different ways in which women and men, girls and boys, look and behave, and how they relate to each other. When we talk about 'gender', we are talking about our society, not about our bodies.

For example, look at the remarks at the beginning of this chapter. It seems that our society expects girls and boys to behave differently. How true is this? Why do we think that a 'real little boy' should be tough, but that a little girl is 'pretty'? Most of the time we just accept remarks like these without thinking. Sometimes we protest that they are unfair or untrue. For example, do women really have difficulty making up their minds, or does this just describe some women or some men? And are all men practical?

The fact is that women and men look and behave differently in different societies. For example, in Western countries, men normally wear trousers. Wearing a skirt or dress is regarded as very odd. But in Egypt, men commonly wear a long cotton robe called a *galabiyah*, especially if they work in the fields. In the cities, many men wear shirts and trousers, but at home they wear a *galabiyah,* because it is cool and relaxing.

As the world around us changes, so do our ideas about gender. Today, in the West, women usually have the choice of wearing dresses and skirts, or trousers. A century ago, women wore only dresses and skirts, usually long and making it difficult for them to move. As women's lives became more interesting and active (as their 'gender roles' changed), so their choice of clothes has become much more varied and suitable.

In Western countries few men would wear a dress or skirt but in Egypt many men, like the one above, prefer to wear the traditional robe, the *galabiyah*.

In most societies, women have been regarded as having less value and less importance than men. This has meant that they have had less chance of getting an education or a good job, of owning land or property, and have had less control over their lives than men.

Our experience of change is affected by many things – our ethnic or racial group, our ideas and religious beliefs, and whether we are rich or poor. Sometimes change takes place very slowly. But in the twentieth century, changes have been so great and have happened so rapidly that their impact has been enormous. This means our lives often turn out differently than we expect.

(Right) In the nineteenth century women and men dressed very differently from each other. Women's clothes were often heavy and uncomfortable.

Changing traditional roles

To show how change affects gender roles in different societies, let us look at the lives of two young couples – Bupe and Malenga in Zambia and Maureen and George in Britain. Both couples have had to rethink the pattern of their lives.

Bupe and Malenga once lived together in their village in western Zambia. Their life followed a traditional path. As a woman, Bupe's job was to grow the family's food, to collect water and fuel, and to care for their children. Malenga also worked on the land, doing 'men's work' – tending animals and growing crops for sale. This pattern changed when Malenga left to work in the copper mines, far away from the village. The wages were

MEDIA WATCH

In January 1995 a court in Britain said that a man who had been dismissed from his job after wearing a skirt to work had not been discriminated against. For eight years the man had worn women's clothing, including leggings and blouses, to work.

In his defence the man said that women were allowed to wear traditional men's clothing, including suits, trousers, shirts and ties, and that his dress was equally appropriate. However, his employers said that the issue was about 'dressing appropriately in a businesslike organization.'

The man's wife said, 'It is unusual for a man to wear a skirt, but there have to be pioneers in every field.'

Do you think that the tribunal made the correct decision? What do we mean by 'appropriate dress' for men and for women?

Source: *The Independent*, 28 January 1995.

good and he regularly sent money home. But he returned only once, or perhaps twice, each year. Other young men left, leaving many women to farm the land and bring up the children alone. The women joined together to help each other, especially

In Zambia, many men leave their villages to work in the copper mines and the industries that have grown around them.

at harvest-time. But life was often very hard. Soon afterwards the Zambian government began encouraging local farmers to grow rice, which could be sold for a higher price than other crops. But rice growing meant much more work, especially weeding and ploughing. If the village women were to benefit, they had to learn new ways of working. This was difficult because the first instructors who arrived to teach the new skills were men. They didn't want to teach the women, saying that women were not 'real' farmers like the men.

But the women were determined to learn. They formed women's groups so that they could support each other. They organized women-only training courses, using practical methods such as discussions and on-the-spot demonstrations, because most women hadn't attended school. The hardest part was learning how to plough. Many villagers said that ploughing was 'men's work' and that a woman's touch would bring bad luck. But when a woman instructor offered to teach the village women to plough, they decided to go ahead. Quietly, they began to practise steering the heavy iron plough behind the oxen. At the next agricultural show, Bupe and the other women demonstrated their ploughing skills to the surprised onlookers.

Today, despite the attitudes of the men, many women farmers successfully grow rice. Even though times are

hard, Bupe manages to provide for her family. But for Malenga, life has become more difficult. After he lost his job in the copper mine, he drifted into casual work, and he can no longer afford to send money to Bupe. He knows that if he went back to live in the villiage, their life would never return to the old ways.

Maureen and George also live in a small village, this time in the north of England. George is a 'househusband'. When anyone asks, he says he works at home. After Maureen leaves for work, George takes care of their two children, cleans, cooks and shops. When he has any spare time he uses it to study electronics with a home-study course.

In many parts of sub-Saharan Africa women do most of the agricultural work. These women in Zimbabwe are harvesting maize. (See also table on page 48).

Like Malenga, George used to be a miner. It was hard work but the money wasn't bad and George thought he would have a job for the rest of his life. But in 1992, after the government began closing many coal mines, George and thousands of other miners lost their jobs. George tried hard to get another job, but unemployment was high and there were no jobs for miners. He had some savings but there were many bills to pay, especially with a new baby. Before their second child was born, Maureen had worked part-time at a bank in the nearby city. Together, Maureen and George decided that Maureen would return to her job full-time, and George would stay at home.

The decision made good sense money-wise, but it was not easy for George to get used to his new role. He felt that a man should support his wife and family. His friends from the former coal mine laughed at him: 'Yer a big sissy,' they said, 'minding bairns [children]. That's women's work.' George felt out of place in other ways, such as attending the 'mother and baby' clinic and the 'mother and toddler' playgroup. He was nearly always the only man there.

George has enjoyed being with his children, seeing them grow and develop. But life was not as easy as he thought it would be. He had never realized how difficult it is to carry shopping and push a baby stroller, while trying to entertain an inquisitive toddler. Although he did not mind a bit of housework, he really did not want to do it every day.

Traditionally coal mining has been a man's job but as many mines in Britain closed, men have had to find different jobs or face unemployment.

Life has changed for Maureen, too. There's much more pressure on her now because the household depends entirely on her wage, but she will never earn as much as George did in the mine. She wishes she could spend more time with the children, and on the weekends she feels she ought to do extra cooking and cleaning. But she also enjoys her work and the sense of achievement it gives her.

Bupe and Malenga, and Maureen and George have changed their traditional gender roles. They did so because outside forces (like the economy and the government) affected their lives, and they made positive decisions to cope with those changes.

In this book we will try to show how gender affects every aspect of our lives: in our homes, our families, in school and at work. We will find that most – but not all – societies regard girls and women as being of less value and less important than boys and men. By looking at the experiences of women and men from many countries and societies, we show how gender roles are changing.

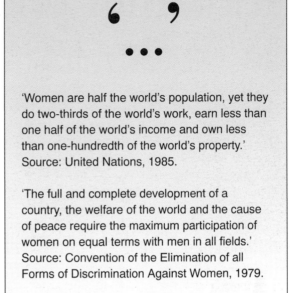

'Women are half the world's population, yet they do two-thirds of the world's work, earn less than one half of the world's income and own less than one-hundredth of the world's property.'
Source: United Nations, 1985.

'The full and complete development of a country, the welfare of the world and the cause of peace require the maximum participation of women on equal terms with men in all fields.'
Source: Convention of the Elimination of all Forms of Discrimination Against Women, 1979.

We men may have 99% of the world's property, earn 90% of the world's income and work ⅔ as many hours as you, but.. you'll LIVE longer!

Is longevity a major cause for celebration under the circumstances?

In Britain, many unemployed men have found new opportunities to spend time with their children.

ALL IN THE FAMILY

Our families give us our first lessons in what it means to be female or male, what is expected of us and how we should behave. And because families are changing, our gender roles – the roles played by girls and boys, women and men – are changing with them.

Extended families

There are many different types of family. An 'extended family' contains not only parents and children, but grandparents, aunts, uncles, cousins, or more distant relatives. Extended families are often found in areas where people work on the land. They help families to survive the bad times (such as poor harvests) and also to provide security for children and older people.

The Mosuo people, who live in a remote part of south-west China, have a very unusual type of extended family, arranged around mothers and daughters. The Mosuo are a tribal people with their own language and way of life. Tseta, a twelve-year-old boy, lives in Luoshui village with his grandmother, his mother and his younger sister, and his mother's brother. Tseta's grandmother is the head of the household and makes the important decisions. Tseta's mother and father have never married and do not live together, but they have a good relationship and Tseta's father is a regular visitor. After Tseta was born, his mother stayed in her own mother's house. Tseta's father stayed with his mother in another village, earning money to support his sister's children. One day, Tseta will do the same.

Among the Mosuo people, this is the traditional way. But it is very different from most Chinese families. In the early 1970s, the Chinese government tried to change the way the Mosuo lived, forcing couples to marry and to live together with their children. But the Mosuo were happy with the old ways. Today the government is more sympathetic and many Mosuo are returning to their traditional extended families.

Large extended families are common where people work on the land. This family comes from West Samoa in the Pacific Ocean.

Nuclear families

In Western societies we are more familiar with a 'nuclear family', where a mother, father and children live together. Nuclear families are often found after people move to live in cities. This process is called 'urbanization' and it is happening all over the world.

Urbanization affects the size of families and the gender roles within them. Look at the lives of Consuelo and José, a couple in Mexico. Both were born in small villages in the southern state of Oaxaca and come from large families. Today they have three children and live in Netzahualcóyati, a sprawling township on the edge of Mexico City. José migrated to the city as a young man, hearing that there were good jobs there. He worked as a cook, a gardener and a driver. Somehow he

A nuclear family, where mother, father and their children live together in one household.

(Right) Millions of people have migrated from the countryside to Mexico City to seek work. They settle in the outskirts of the city, often building their homes on waste land.

managed to finish high school at night and then did a course in electrical repairing. At first José hoped to save enough money to return to his village, but later he decided to stay. He had grown used to city life.

Consuelo came to Mexico City to join her elder sister. Like her sister, Consuelo first worked as a maid, then in a factory because the pay was better. She did not have enough education to become an office worker, where the pay was better still. Later, she became a trader, cooking food at home and selling it in the market. Consuelo also joined the local neighbourhood association, campaigning for facilities like running water, electricity and a rubbish collection. All the volunteers were women.

Consuelo and José moved to Netzahualcóyati because it was easier to find land there and build a small house. In the following years, four children were born, two girls and two boys. One of the boys died when he was a few days old. After the last birth, Consuelo and José decided that three children were enough. Although Consuelo and José made the decision together, it was Consuelo who felt more strongly about it. Her own mother had borne nine children and had spent most of her life cooking and cleaning and being pregnant. Consuelo did not want this life for herself.

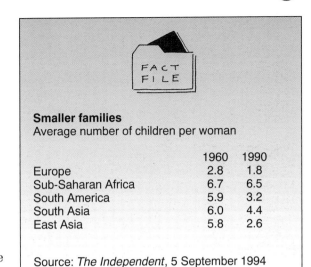

Smaller families
Average number of children per woman

	1960	1990
Europe	2.8	1.8
Sub-Saharan Africa	6.7	6.5
South America	5.9	3.2
South Asia	6.0	4.4
East Asia	5.8	2.6

Source: *The Independent*, 5 September 1994

Family planning

Consuelo had already heard a lot about family planning. She had talked with the women in the community association, and with the midwife who had delivered her children and was also a family planning advisor. Consuelo learnt about the different types of contraception – oral contraceptive pills, condoms, and sterilization. Finally she decided that sterilization was the most suitable birth control method for her. Consuelo had to get José's permission to have the sterilization operation. At first he was reluctant. He felt that he would be less of a man if there were no more children. When he was a boy his father had made all the important decisions. But after talking it over, he realized how strongly Consuelo felt and he agreed to give his permission.

Consuelo and José chose to have only three children because they wanted to give them a good start in life, and a good education. Although city wages are higher

Some governments promote family planning through advertising. This Chinese poster asks couples to have only one child.

than in Oaxaca, prices are also higher, especially for housing. Life is more hectic in the city and there are fewer family members – mothers, grandmothers, aunts – to help out. And in Mexico, prices keep rising.

Consuelo and José's decision to have a smaller family is not unusual. It is a trend all over the world. Consuelo and José were lucky because the Mexican government supports family planning and the clinic was close by. The situation is different in many other countries.

One-parent families

Another common type of family is the 'one-parent family'. In nine out of ten cases, this parent is the mother, so these families are often called 'woman-headed households'. The numbers of woman-headed households are increasing all over the world. There are many reasons why this is so. Wars and conflicts separate families through death or migration. More women are having children outside marriage, sometimes out of choice but also because men may decide that supporting a wife and children is too difficult or too expensive.

In the past, extended families and social pressures often kept married couples together, but today those pressures are not so strong and in most countries, divorce rates are rising. For example, each year in the USA, one million children see their parents get divorced.

In many countries women are left to bring up children alone because war and migration force families apart. This family is from Zambia.

Family planning often focuses on women. Ideally men should also be involved.

Many women decide that they no longer want to remain married, especially when they have been badly treated. But the price of freedom is often poverty and hardship.

In many parts of the world, men leave home to find work, leaving the women to take care of the children, as happened to Bupe in Zambia. Left behind, the women have

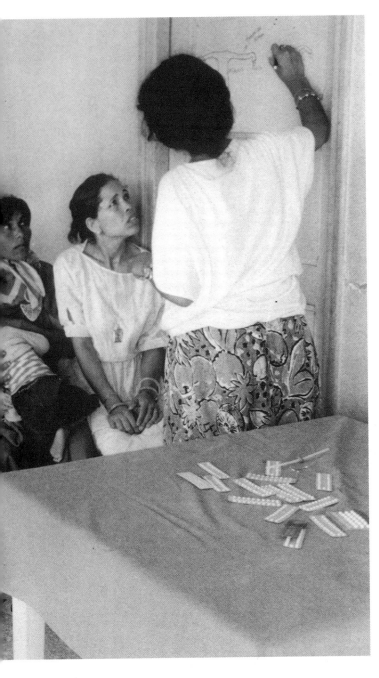

The right to contraception
Women say they want greater choice over the number and spacing of their children. However, many face great difficulties in receiving either advice or contraception.

Worldwide, it is estimated that there are 300 million women who want to use contraception but cannot. This may be because governments do not want to make contraceptives easily available, or because a woman's partner will not allow it.

Although it is relatively easy to obtain contraception in most Western countries, many teenagers still find it difficult to receive reliable information about sex, pregnancy, sexually transmitted diseases, and contraception.

to struggle on as best they can. It can be difficult for a parent to raise a family alone, trying to give children the attention they need, take care of a home and make a living. The biggest problem that woman-headed households face is poverty. On average, they are twice as likely to be poor as households having two parents.

FACT FILE

Woman-headed households as a percentage of the total number of households

Europe	20
Sub-Saharan Africa	30
Asia	20
USA	23
South America	30
Caribbean	30

Source: *People and Planet,* vol 2 no 3, 1994.

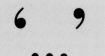

Sons or daughters?
In many countries, parents say that they would prefer to have a son rather than a daughter. This is because a son will carry on the family name and contribute to the family wealth. For example in rural areas of Jordan, a boy's birth is announced by saying 'God sent the family a farmer.' A girl's arrival is announced by saying 'God sent the family a bride' [who will go away].

All over the world, families are undergoing change. People will always argue about which type of family is best. But in the end, being a good parent is about giving children love and security, and this can be done in many ways and in many different types of families.

Lesbian parents with their child (see page 35).

BRIDGING THE GAP

Hu Bangjing wants to be a teacher. She is twelve years old, and she lives alone in a village in the poor province of Guizhou in China. Every day Hu Bangjing gets up, tends to the pigs, and then attends school for nine hours. She tries to study in the evenings, but it is difficult because the light is poor and she is tired and often hungry. Her school gives her a tracksuit to wear as a uniform and her mother, Zhou Yuhua, visits her once each week, bringing as much food as she can spare. Otherwise she must manage by herself.

Education can bring independence and girls in China are keen to learn.

Hu Bangjing's life is different from that of most other girls in China. Her father died when she was a baby. When Hu Bangjing's mother remarried, her new

husband was happy to welcome her son, but said he
wouldn't accept ten-year-old Hu Bangjing, because
'boys are wealth but girls are a burden'. So Hu Bangjing
lives alone and studies hard. If she becomes a teacher,
she will earn as much in one month as a poor farmer
can earn in a year, and will be given a room to live in at
the local school.

For a poor girl like Hu Bangjing, education can bring
independence. Teachers are respected because of their
learning. Hu Bangjing will no longer be regarded as a
burden when she becomes a teacher. She will not have
to marry a farmer and work the fields, but can choose
her own husband. If her husband dies or leaves her, she
will be able to support herself and her children.

Education for a better life

There are many people throughout the world who are
prepared to give up a lot to be able to learn. Like Hu
Bangjing, they know that education can be the way to a
better life. If they are poor, they believe that it will help
them get a better job. But girls in particular may have to

Serious business: girls at
this secondary school in
Ghana are determined to
learn.

This Bolivian woman works as a technician at Radio San Gabriel in La Paz. Learning computer skills helps women to compete with men for a wider variety of jobs.

struggle in order to learn. Even if they start school, they might have to drop out in order to help with the housework and look after younger children. And when education is expensive, as it is in many countries, families have to choose between sending a boy to school or a girl. They usually choose the boy, because boys are seen to be more important to their family's future. A girl will get married and leave, whereas a boy will stay and look after his parents in their old age.

FACT FILE

Older women learn in Bolivia

Women in Bolivia, in South America, wanted to be able to read what their children had written, understand prices and shop signs, and booklets on health and childcare. So a number of groups were set up to teach women to read. These are proving very successful. As Margarita, a woman in one of the groups, put it: 'The faster we women learn, the quicker we can liberate ourselves.'

One literacy class in La Paz, the capital of Bolivia, showed very clearly how reading and writing were linked to action. The class was split into two groups: the women who still could not read and write were sitting inside together learning to write their names. Meanwhile, outside, a second group of women who could already read were debating how to persuade the men to move the rubbish outside their homes in order to prevent the spread of disease.

Boys in the front row: here in Sri Lanka, as elsewhere, boys are more likely than their sisters to get an education.

Worldwide, at primary level, 82 per cent of boys and 71 per cent of girls go to school (although this varies a lot from country to country). Primary school is often paid for by the government, and the number of children attending went up a lot in the 1980s. But at secondary school level, only half of all children go to school – and once again there are more boys than girls. On average, by the time a girl is eighteen, she will have received 4.4 years less education than a boy. There are still 900 million people in the world over the age of fifteen who cannot read or write and 600 million of these are women.

FACT FILE

Percentage of students attending secondary school 1987

	Boys	Girls
Sub-Saharan Africa	32	15
Middle East	57	41
South America and the Caribbean	52	56
East Asia	50	39
South Asia	44	25

Source: UNESCO, 1990

(Right) More girls are now studying science, once considered to be a 'male' subject.

The trouble with boys

Recent reports in the media suggest that although there is often a gap between the education of boys and of girls, in Britain this seems to be closing. Girls are overtaking boys in subjects that were once considered boys' subjects – maths, science and technology. This appears to be because girls work harder and take their work much more seriously.

A report in *The Independent* in October 1994 is typical: Paul Cavanagh, aged seventeen, is honest about why he did worse than he expected in his exams. 'Complacency and arrogance,' he says. 'After our mock exams, the teachers predicted I would get six grade "A"s. No trouble, I thought, I don't need to work. So I didn't, and I only got three "A"s.'

Paul is now in the sixth form. He says he is working hard to get to a decent university, but still not as hard as the girls in his physics year. 'The group is nearly all boys. They do almost no work at all, especially homework,' he says.

Paul, according to national studies, is a typical male student. Girls work harder and are less confident of their abilities. Working hard is not 'cool' for either sex, but girls are less swayed by their peers' attitude to schoolwork.

Think about whether the girls at your school work harder than the boys and why this might be?

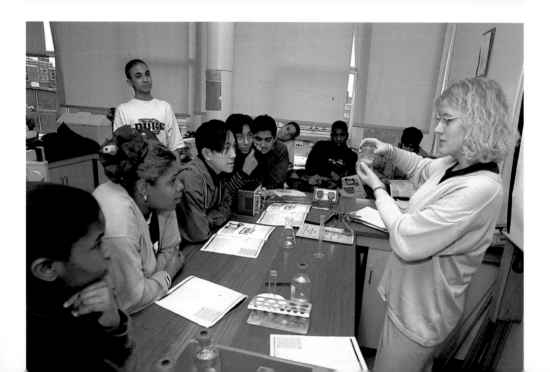

Children at playschool in Bangladesh – but will the girls get the chance to go on to school?

Education for change

Sayeeda Begum cannot read or write. She lives in a village in Bangladesh. Sayeeda has had a very hard life. Married at fourteen, having worked all her life in the fields, at forty she thinks her life is over. She has borne seven children, of whom five have survived – three girls and two boys. Sayeeda's neighbours say that it would have been better if more boys had lived, because boys are a support in old age whereas girls will get married and leave. Also, when girls get married, a

dowry has to be found to pay the bridegroom. There is a saying in Bangladesh: 'Educating your daughter is like watering another man's fields.' For every six children enrolled in primary school, only one is a girl. Despite this, Sayeeda Begum knew that education was the key to her daughters' future. Although she felt that it was too late for her to learn to read and write, she was determined that Razia, Sakina and five-year-old Rukaya would have more chances in life than she did. At first she feared that she would not be able to afford to have all her children educated. Then one day, Sayeeda's husband, Taib, came back from a visit to a nearby village with the news that a school was being set up. It seemed to be aimed especially at them – poor people who worked on other people's fields. And what was more, it was mainly for girls.

Over the next few years, Sayeeda found out much more about BRAC (the Bangladesh Rural Advancement Committee), the organization that was starting the school. BRAC schools provide three years of basic education for each child at a low cost to the family. Because the schools recognize the difficulties of girls getting an education, 70 per cent of the children are girls. Classes are small, and the timetable and school year fit in with the farming season.

The nearest BRAC school was close enough for Sayeeda and Taib's three daughters to be able to walk there. They loved it. For two and a half hours a day they studied, and were back in time to help their parents at home and in the fields.

Today, the two eldest girls are doing as well as their brothers. They both hope to go on to secondary school, and then Razia wants to go back and be a BRAC teacher. There are now 6,000 BRAC schools, and more are planned, so she should have plenty of choice. Sakina wants to become a village health worker. Meanwhile, all the children are able to help their parents at home and in the fields, as well as studying.

Sayeeda was right in wanting her daughters as well as her sons to go to school. It has been proved time and time again that sending girls to school is not only good for the girl, but gives her and her future family a better chance in life and a higher standard of living. A woman in India once said: 'If you educate a man you educate a person; if you educate a woman you educate a family'. Women who have been to school are likely to get married later, have fewer children, and know more about health – and so have healthier families. It has been shown that even a few years of education make a difference.

Returning home from school in Barbados: education is the key to these children's future.

Because of their schooling, Hu Bangjing and Razia, Sakina and little Rukaya will have more chance than their mothers to improve their lives, and to bridge the gap between them and their brothers. In doing this, they will help their own families, their villages and the whole society in which they live.

(Right) Young people get to know each in school in the USA.

GETTING TOGETHER

All around the world, young people find ways of meeting and enjoying each other's company. They do this in many ways. What is acceptable in one society might be unthinkable in another, and what is considered normal behaviour for a boy might be condemned in a girl. Let us look at some young people in two very different societies.

An arranged marriage
Sayeed, who is sixteen, lives with his family in a city in Pakistan. He knows that one day he will marry

Young people and their families enjoying a day out on a beach in Karachi, Pakistan.

Which sex?
When the sperm from the father joins the egg of the mother, they produce an embryo, which grows in the mother's womb and eventually becomes a baby. All the information that makes us unique (different from anyone else) goes into forty-six chromosomes. Two chromosomes, called X and Y, make the difference between male or female. Males have an X and a Y chromosome, females have two X chromosomes.

After about six weeks, male embryos start producing a hormone (growth substance) called testosterone, to begin developing what we call 'male characteristics'. Female development is guided by a different hormone, called oestrogen.

fourteen-year-old Fatima, who is a distant cousin. Their two families arranged it many years ago. He has only seen Fatima a couple of times at big family occasions, and he has never actually talked to her, but he can see that she is very pretty. He is very happy to let his family choose his wife: that is the way things are usually organized in Pakistan.

Fatima is also happy. Her family has told her good things about Sayeed, and, after all, he is family. She is pleased that the wedding will wait until both she and Sayeed have finished school. Unlike her mother, who married at fifteen, she will have an education, although she knows that the most important thing is that she should have a son, or maybe two or three. When she has her first son, then she really will be grown up.

In the meantime, Sayeed has quite a lot of freedom. He travels to school by himself, and in the evening he hangs around the teashops and cinemas with his friends. Fatima is much more restricted. When she leaves the house she must be accompanied by a male relative or another woman, and for the last two years she has had to cover her head with a large shawl when she goes out so that strange men cannot see her face.

The freedom to choose

David also lives in a big city, this time in Australia. He has just turned fifteen and he finds girls almost as interesting as he finds football. He and his mates spend quite a bit of time talking about girls – which ones they fancy and how to attract them. It can be hard going, especially as the girls in his class are a lot more interested in older boys. There is a lot of boasting about sex, but David thinks most of the boys are like him and have not yet had sex with a girl.

How does David see his future? He guesses that one day he will get married and have a family, but not for years, maybe not until he is twenty-five or thirty. First he has got to finish school; then he wants a good job, a place of his own, and a chance to travel overseas. And, of course, he would like to meet lots of girls. He does not want to get a girl pregnant, but when it comes to contraception he thinks that the main responsibility is

Young women and men in America meet together informally and on equal terms at college.

hers, not his. On the other hand, he's heard quite a lot about AIDS and safe sex, so he will think about using condoms – if he remembers.

Some of the girls in David's class have already got steady boyfriends and cannot wait to settle down. Most girls prefer to look around, to 'play the field.' Like David, they want to wait until they are in their twenties before they decide on marriage and children. Some say that they do not want to get married at all – they do not believe that marriage is a fair deal for women. Better to have a good job they say – you can rely on that.

In Western countries teenagers enjoy leisure time with friends of both sexes.

Finding a place to meet privately can sometimes be hard. These teenagers get together in a park.

Equal terms?

Big differences you may think. But these young people from Pakistan and Australia have more in common than at first appears. For example, both Sayeed and David have more time and freedom, and less responsibility, than girls of a similar age. Fatima faces the greatest restrictions, but even in Australia parents are likely to be more concerned for a daughter's safety than for a son's. In both countries, girls are expected to help with household tasks; boys not so often, or never.

If Fatima and Sayeed fail to have children, and especially if there are no sons, it is Fatima who will be blamed, not Sayeed. He could divorce Fatima and send her back to her family in disgrace. If her marriage is happy, if Sayeed's

FACT FILE

Same sex attraction

It is common to have sexual feelings towards a person of the same sex as ourselves.
If this attraction is very intense, it is called homosexuality. Homosexual men are known as 'gays' and homosexual women as 'lesbians'. We do not know why some people are heterosexual and others homosexual, but we do know that it happens in every society, even though gays and lesbians may be ignored or treated badly.

family care for her, if she has sons – then she will have more chance to make her views heard, especially as she grows older.

In Australia, a girl has to treat sex and contraception much more seriously than a boy. If she becomes pregnant, she may have to choose between an abortion or bringing up a baby alone. A baby means fewer opportunities for education, work and fun. And there are still double standards: it is easy for a girl to get a bad reputation if she is thought to be 'sleeping around', while a boy doing the same thing is usually regarded as a 'stud'.

But things are changing. Young women face the world with increasing confidence. They believe that both sexes should be treated equally, at school, at home and in their social life. Young men are beginning to realize that they also have to adapt to a world in which women have a greater role to play.

Today, more than ever, girls and boys are beginning to meet on equal terms. But let us look at what happens when they go out to work.

In Western countries young people may travel widely before they settle down. This young woman is hiking through the mountains of Bulgaria.

GOING OUT TO WORK

Rosa and Jim have Saturday jobs at their local store. Although they are both the same age and study the same subjects at school, in the supermarket they were placed in different jobs. Rosa became a checkout girl and Jim an assistant packer.

Many jobs are divided on gender lines. Store checkout operators are generally women; store managers are mainly men.

It didn't take Rosa long to learn the basics of her checkout job. A lot is done by automated machinery. A bar code on each item is passed under an electronic eye, and the price appears automatically on the computerized cash register, which calculates the total and produces a detailed receipt. The human part is handling the money – cash, cheques, credit cards – and giving change. The quicker the machines can work, the more pressure there is on the operator to work harder and faster, to serve more and more customers. It is also very boring. Rosa has to stay in her checkout area and can only take a break at certain fixed times.

Jim's job is no more skilled than Rosa's but he moves around more. He helps to unload and unpack goods, stack shelves, run

errands and, when queues are long, helps on the checkouts. It is easier to take a break, to stop for a chat or a laugh, than it is for Rosa on her checkout.

Gender divisions

If Rosa and Jim have the same education and abilities, why were they offered different jobs? The store manager (a man) says: 'You can't put boys on the checkouts for too long. They get restless, slow down, they aren't so good with people. They like to move around. The girls are better at the fiddly work and better with people. And the boys' work takes strength. It's not very feminine to lift heavy boxes, is it?' (Actually, in most big stores, moving goods does not involve heavy lifting.)

The work in the store is divided according to gender lines. It is mainly boys and men who unpack and shelve goods, working in the evenings after the store has closed. The checkout operators are girls and

In England women were allowed to become priests in the Anglican church in 1994. In one year over 1,000 women were ordained as Anglican priests.

It is only relatively recently that women in Britain, such as this bus driver, have been allowed to work in 'male' jobs.

Equal opportunities?
'The barrier between men and women at work remains as entrenched as ever', according to a report of the Equal Opportunities Commission in March 1995. The Commission believes that gender division in work places and jobs is striking.

Administrative and clerical workers tend to be women, but skilled workers, senior professional, technical and managerial staff tend to be men. Gender division can lead to discrimination, mainly in recruitment, promotion and pay.

The report says that women working with other women tended to be paid less, while men working with other men received higher salaries. Employers are unaware or not worried by the problem.

women: 'casuals' at weekends, and older women on weekdays. Some work 'flexible hours' – different times on different days. Because the store now stays open longer, hours have become even more flexible and there are more women working part-time. Nearly all the managers are men, although a few women supervise the checkout operators and other 'female' jobs.

Rosa knows the situation is unfair, but for the moment she is not too worried. She sees her future quite differently, in getting good grades at school and further qualifications at college. That way she should be able to go for the job she wants and compete on equal terms with men.

Women train alongside men at this US Marines training camp.

Yet Rosa may well be disappointed. The fact is most jobs and professions are divided according to gender.

Almost every job has a gender image attached to it. In general, the jobs we think of as being more active and interesting, more productive and creative, more concerned with planning and managing people, are seen as 'men's work'. The jobs which are seen as more passive and routine, more detailed and inward looking, more concerned with people and their needs, are considered 'women's work'.

Sometimes women enter 'male' jobs. For example, look at the medical profession. Traditionally we think of a doctor as a 'male' job and a nurse as a 'female' job. Worldwide, most doctors are men and the overwhelming majority of nurses are women. As more women qualify as doctors, some of these images are changing. Even so, the long working hours place extra pressures on women doctors, especially if they are trying to juggle work and a family. One result is that men are more likely to become surgeons and hospital specialists, while women become 'family doctors'.

FACT FILE

Women at work

Percentage of the paid workforce who are women

	1970	1993
Europe	36.3	39.5
Sub-Saharan Africa	40.6	38.1
Former USSR	51.1	48.8
North America	36.2	41.3
South America	21.6	27.0
South Asia	25.0	21.9

Source: *The Guardian,* 27 April, 1994.

And although more men are entering nursing, it is still seen as a good job for women because they can combine it more easily with family life.

Equal rights?

For women, many aspects of work have changed for the better, particularly in Western countries. There is a wider choice of jobs, especially for educated women. Many countries have passed laws that give women more rights at work. These include being paid the same amount of

(Left) These were the first women to work for a Kuwaiti oil company. One is wearing traditional clothing, the other is wearing Western clothes.

money for doing the same job as a man. But when jobs are divided according to gender, it can be difficult to decide what 'equal pay' really means.

Worldwide, more and more women now work for money, in factories and offices, supermarkets and banking. They work because they have to support themselves and their families. But most of these jobs are still classified as 'female' and many women workers are paid very little – certainly less than a man would be paid. They may have little protection from their employers, and few rights. They may face sexual harassment by male workers, or they may not be paid when they are ill or when their children are sick.

Many women work in offices – but generally as secretaries rather than managers.

In some countries, women hold down important jobs, particularly in the 'caring professions', such as

education, health and welfare. But other areas remain unchanged, particularly at the highest levels. Women often say that they have to work much harder than men to reach the same positions, and that they have to make more sacrifices – for example, not having children, or not spending as much time with them as they would like.

Management is still seen as a 'male' job. Because it is easier to work with people like oneself, male managers are likely to promote other men to top posts rather than women. Of the 1,000 largest US companies, only two were headed by a woman.

Men can do 'female' jobs just as well as women. This Australian man works as a 'home help'.

In other parts of the world, women workers are losing rights. Unemployment has affected men as well as women, but when there are not many full-time paid jobs around, they are often given to men.

Take Irina, who is a teacher living with her family in Moscow, the capital of Russia. When Irina was small, her mother was a teacher and her father an engineer. She and her sister attended a local free nursery. The family were not rich but they managed.

Today, Irina is the only one in her family still working. She does not earn enough to live on herself, let alone support the whole family. Irina's job is not safe because she is a woman. A Russian government minister made

Divided by gender
Although all of the jobs listed below can be done equally well by either women or men, we normally think of them as 'female' or 'male'.

female	male
nurse	doctor
interior designer	architect
secretary	executive assistant
departmental secretary	manager
fashion journalist	sports journalist
sales assistant	travelling representative
filing clerk	mechanic
primary school teacher	lecturer
waitress	chef

this very clear when he said: 'Why should we employ women when men are unemployed?' More and more women in Russia are losing their jobs, and their right to free childcare, education and unemployment benefit. Irina is very worried about the future.

The future
Let us return to Rosa and Jim who both work in their local store. What will their future be? The chances are that both will end up working in jobs divided by gender. However, Rosa has a better chance of escaping a dead-end job than her mother's generation did. For one thing she has more legal rights to protect her; for another, she is more likely to keep working all or most of her adult life, perhaps taking a few years' break if she has children.

For Jim, there is a different dilemma – because many 'male' jobs are disappearing. He may have to take a number of different jobs during his life. This means he will have to learn to be flexible, and consider jobs that were formerly classed as 'female'. But it is unlikely that he will have the main responsibility for childcare. As the next chapter shows, that is still mainly seen as a woman's task.

Women are breaking into jobs formerly regarded as 'male', like this trainee window cleaner in San Francisco, USA.

THE DOUBLE DAY

Mboja yawns and stretches, and then slips out of bed, quietly, so as not to wake her sleeping brothers and sisters. Outside, the trees are outlined darkly against the sky. But Mboja pays little attention to the beauty beyond the courtyard of her home in Tanzania. It is five o'clock in the morning, and she is already late.

Mboja arranges the wood that took her two hours to gather the night before, and lights a fire. Then she struggles to lift the heavy iron pot from its resting-place and heaves it on top of the heat. In go the ingredients. A quick wash, and the children are woken. Stubborn and complaining, they stumble about their daily tasks. They still miss their mother, who died nine months

These women farmers in Uganda are working together to pull up the root vegetable, cassava. After they finish, they still have work to do at home.

ago, and grumble at their elder sister, who has had to take on all her mother's tasks. By seven o'clock the house has been swept, breakfast eaten, and Mboja's other work begins. As the sun rises, she sets off for the fields.

Far away in Cairo, the capital of Egypt, an alarm clock goes off. Samia groans and gets out of bed. It is still dark, and she pads quietly to the bathroom before switching on the light. Her husband is asleep. She dresses and prepares breakfast for him and for her mother-in-law and niece, and snatches some flat bread and olives and a glass of sweet tea. Then she lets herself quietly out of the house and hails a taxi.

What do both Mboja in Tanzania and Samia in Egypt have in common with women the world over? They are both up early, earlier than either the men or the children, in order to do the jobs at home before they start on their 'other' work – the work that helps pay for them and their families to live. They all work a double day – going out to earn money, but having to care for their families before and after work.

Mboja has the longest day. This is partly because she lives in the countryside. In addition to cooking and preparing food, cleaning, looking after the children and animals, she has to do all the work that any other farmer does – weeding, harvesting, planting and selling. Her father helps with the ploughing and the planting, but most of the work and all of the childcare is done by Mboja.

The double day worked by many women in the African countryside has become much harder over the last few years. This is partly because farmers get less money than before for their crops, while at the same time everything they need to buy has become more expensive. It is also because of environmental problems. The cutting down of trees, for example, means that women have to walk further to fetch firewood. And at the same time, more women have to run their households alone because men have had to leave in search of jobs.

FACT FILE

Parents' leave
A large number of countries allow women time off work to have their babies. This is called maternity leave. It is more difficult for fathers to get paternity leave.

• In Japan the law allows women sixteen weeks' maternity leave, although this is sometimes unpaid.

• In Burkina Faso, trade unions have made an agreement for mothers to receive social security during their three months' maternity leave.

• The European Union (fifteen countries) passed laws in 1994 to allow new fathers to take three months' unpaid leave when their babies are born. The British government said that this would cost too much and refused to accept it.

Because Samia lives in the city, she has different problems from Mboja, who lives in the countryside. In some ways, Samia and her husband are lucky. They both work in Egypt's civil service, so they earn quite a lot of money and even pay for someone else to do some of the work in the house. But it is always Samia who is responsible for the household. If they have children, she will also look after them, though her mother-in-law will help.

Like Samia, Arianna lives in a city. This time it is Athens in Greece. Arianna and her husband Stavros both work in a bank. Before their daughter was born, Arianna and Stavros did the same well-paid job organizing computer systems. When Arianna applied for the job six years ago, she knew that the work was thought of as men's work. Not many women applied and still fewer passed the test, but she felt she could do it and she did.

At first everything was fine. The bank provided excellent training for the men and the few women whom they had taken on, although the work was hard. Both Arianna and Stavros often had to come in at very short notice, and work long hours far from home, helping the 500 different branches throughout the country to install new computers.

The myth of the 'New Man'
A newspaper report suggested that American men are sharing more childcare duties with their partners. Yet a new study shows that American women average 10.7 hours each weekday caring for pre-school children, while fathers take charge without the mothers' help for less than an hour a day on average.

Source: *Los Angeles Times*, February 1995.

Then things changed: Arianna and Stavros got married and had a child, Elena. Arianna could no longer travel for long periods; nor could she go to work at short notice because she had to arrange for her mother to look after Elena. The bank said that there were no other similar jobs that she could do. So she took on a much less responsible and lower-paid job, which fitted in with her various commitments at home.

Arianna knows that even if she returns to her old job when Elena is older, she will never catch up with Stavros. Meanwhile Stavros is doing well at work, but because he works longs hours he sees very little of his daughter.

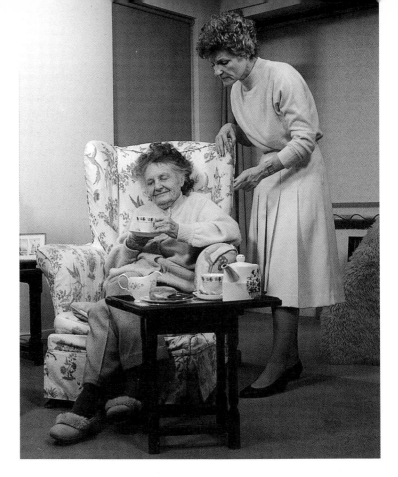

Tea and sympathy, as this woman looks after her elderly mother.

Parents at work

Everywhere in the world, women have to juggle their caring responsibilities with their paid work. Many women care for their elderly parents or older relatives. The vast majority care for their children. Although there are some men (like George in the first chapter) who do most of the childcare, they are still the exceptions. Even in the USA and Australia, where women work the same number of hours as men – though not for the same money or in the same jobs – women still do 75 per cent of the household chores and most of the childcare.

But things are slowly changing. In 1981, the International Labour Organization produced a Convention called 'Workers with family responsibilities'. Those countries that signed it had to promise to try to help parents at work. This applied to men as well as women, recognizing that both should share family responsibilities.

When, in 1993, a special committee was set up to find out what had been done, it found that in many countries changes had been made to help working parents at work. These included flexible working hours, more widespread leave for parents, and better childcare. Where employers made these changes, it meant that fewer people took sick leave, and more were happy with their work and stayed longer in their jobs. This was good for the companies as well as for the employees and their families.

Changing the laws and encouraging employers to make working life easier for all parents is one way of taking the burden of the double day away from women and sharing it out equally. Persuading men to play their part in childcare and home responsibilities is another. But both are important because in the end sharing the burden will benefit everyone – men, women and children, too.

This workplace nursery in Belarus, in the former USSR, helps children, parents and employers.

FACT FILE

In African countries, the way that rural farm work is divided means that women work many more hours than men:

Percentage of work done by women and men

	Women	Men
Domestic work	95	5
Processing and storing crops	85	15
Weeding	70	30
Harvesting	60	40
Caring for animals	50	50
Planting	50	50
Ploughing	30	70

Source: 'Integrating women into development is a myth' by Adelina Ndeto Mwau, in *Changing perceptions: writings on gender and development*, edited by Tina Wallace with Candida March, Oxfam 1991.

SPEAKING UP FOR CHANGE

Mary Robinson, Ireland's first woman president, speaks up for women's causes in Ireland and elsewhere.

When we think of politics, we tend to think of the people we elect to run our government. Today, in almost every country, women have the right to vote on equal terms with men. All over the world, more and more women are choosing to take part in politics at all levels. Some women stand in elections, so that they can play a direct role in government. This can be a long process, taking time, as well as money.

Once it was taken for granted that all politicians were men. Today, there are still more men than women in politics, although women politicians are slowly growing in numbers. Some women reach the highest positions, such as president or prime minister. This has happened in countries as different as Israel, India, Britain, Bangladesh, Norway, Pakistan, Ireland, Poland and Turkey. But their success does not always result in more opportunities for other women.

Politics is not just about running for elections or gaining power. It is also about making changes in

The right to vote
In the nineteenth century, women (called suffragettes) started campaigning for the right to vote. It was a long struggle. Women gained the vote in 1893 in New Zealand and 1901 in Australia but in most countries they had to wait until after the first world war (USA 1920, Britain 1928), or after the second world war (France 1944, Switzerland 1971).

our lives, perhaps by improving our present laws, or gaining new rights, or fighting for the things we care about. Look at these stories of women in politics from three different countries.

The Indian *panchyat*

Indira, who lives in a village in central India, was named after Indira Gandhi, India's only woman prime minister. Two years ago she was elected to the village *panchyat* (council), together with two other women, Amina and Kumari. This was after the Indian government said that every *panchyat* had to have women members. Why were the women elected? They were the wives of the most important men in the village.

When the three women attended their first *panchyat* meeting, they sat apart from the men, not saying a single word. Amina covered her face with her veil and Kumari sat looking at the ground. Indira was a little bolder. She was the only one who could read and she had spent three years at secondary school. She earned a small salary working for a voluntary organization as a community worker. So Indira was used to meeting with the village women and hearing their problems.

One day, some of the poorer women told her the *panchyat* should close the liquor shops outside the village, because their husbands were spending a lot of time and money there. Sometimes, when the men were drunk, they would beat their wives. Indira knew about the liquor shops but she had not taken much notice because they did not affect her. Also, like many other people, she accepted that

women got beaten. But the more Indira heard from the other women, the more she realized that she had to do something about this problem.

The organization Indira worked for held a training course attended by all the women community workers in the district. It seemed that liquor shops were a common problem. And there were others – like the need for clean water and more drugs in the clinic. They discussed the role women played in their communities and why it was wrong for women to be beaten. Finally Indira decided to speak at the *panchyat* meeting. At first she spoke so softly that she could hardly be heard.

In India, and also in neighbouring Bangladesh, women often join together to improve health and family welfare.

'As women we particularly identify with our Mother Earth. We recognize that the Earth is life ... This Mother Earth is the only one that we have: we must respect her, care for her, love her. In every country people are destroying and violating Mother Earth. She is dying, so we the people are dying. We take our responsibility seriously. We defend the Earth.'

From a statement issued by the Women's Commission at the First Continental Meeting of Indigenous Peoples in Quito, Ecuador, July 1990.

She said that the *panchyat* should ban the liquor shops. Most of the men disagreed and so the liquor shops stayed. But Indira slowly became more confident. Now she speaks at every *panchyat* meeting. Although Amina and Kumari are still too shy to speak, they now vote with her, against the liquor shops, and for more money for a clean water supply. Their voices are beginning to make a difference to everyone's lives.

Working women in Brazil

On the other side of the world, Maria is also speaking up for change. Maria lives on a large sugar-cane farm in north-east Brazil. Her parents were so poor that she started working when she was only seven years old. When she was a teenager, Maria married another farmworker and rapidly had four children, all the time continuing to work in the fields.

Maria's husband, Antonio, belonged to the trade union that fought for the rights of farmworkers, but women could only join if their husbands were members. Maria joined a group of women who called themselves *Movimento das Mulheres Trabalhadores* (MMT), which means Working Women's Organization. They campaigned for women to join the union as members in their own right, to take part in union meetings and to receive the same pay as men. Maria wanted paid maternity leave because she knew how cruel and painful it was to give birth at night and then have to return to work in the fields the following day. She feared for her children, left alone at home. What if something happened to them while she was working? MMT called for the sugar-cane company to provide a nursery for the children of the farmworkers.

Maria became involved in politics through MMT. On 8 March, International Women's Day, MMT organized a meeting of women workers – farm and factory workers, schoolteachers, and servants. Together they wrote a list of the things they wanted, the rights they felt they should be given as women, and presented them to the government. As more and more women joined MMT, they began to ask why things could not be more equal in their homes and families. After all, no matter how

Women throughout the world have played a leading role in supporting environmental issues. Here in Hawaii a women's group leads a demonstration to protect the rainforest.

hard they worked, they were still the ones who looked after the children, cooked and cleaned. The men would not help – they said that this was women's work. So MMT began organizing meetings between women and men to try to talk over some of the problems. It took a long time and there is still a long way to go, but, slowly, some of the men are changing their ideas and trying to find more equal ways of living and working.

In Brazil woman and girls want equality at home, work and school.

Discrimination in Zambia
In Zambia, southern Africa, a young woman called Sara Longwe was also fighting for equal rights for women.

(Right) This poster informs Kenyan women where to find help if they are victims of violence.

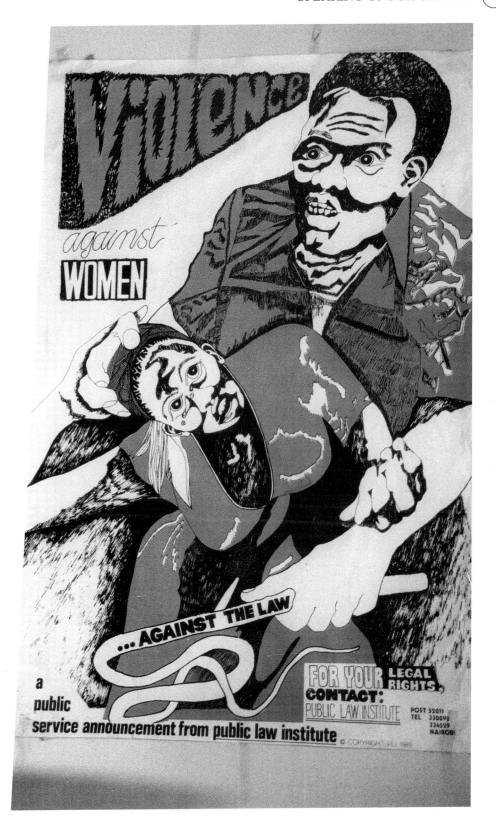

FACT FILE

Domestic violence

Violence against women is a major problem worldwide. For example, each year in the USA, 1,500 women are killed by their husbands and boyfriends. A further 2.5 million women are assaulted, raped or robbed, often by men they know. This kind of attack, which often takes place at home, is called 'domestic violence'. In many countries, feminists have opened refuges, or 'safe houses', for women and children escaping from domestic violence.

Emma Humphreys was only seventeen when she was jailed by an English court for murder. She was freed ten years later (in 1995), after a campaign by her supporters, who argued that she had acted only after being beaten and abused by her violent, drunken partner.

In 1984 she had been refused entry to a hotel in Lusaka, Zambia's capital city. Sara protested when the manager told her that a woman could not come into the hotel unless she was with a man. When the police arrived they told Sara that if she did not 'shut up' they would arrest her.

Sara began a campaign for equal treatment for women. Although modern Zambian law says that women and men have equal rights, under traditional laws, a woman was considered to be a 'minor' (child). She either belonged to her father, if she was single, or to her husband if she was married. The problem was that many organizations, like hotels, still considered a woman to be a man's property.

All over the world young women fight for fair and equal treatment. These Australian students are protesting for a better education.

Finally, Sara began a court case against the hotel, claiming that it was wrong for the hotel to discriminate against women. The case took many years. It was only in 1992 that the High Court of Zambia found that Sara had been discriminated against and said that the hotel should treat women and men equally.

Feminism

In their different ways, Indira, Maria and Sara are all part of a worldwide movement. Some people call this movement feminism – the belief that women and men should be treated equally. There are many different types of feminism, and there is a lot of discussion about the way forward. But all feminists are inspired by the idea of equality. Today there are feminists all over the world, and feminism is one of the strongest influences in the politics of our daily lives. Feminism means that girls and women should have the right to a good education, to the same pay for the same job, and to equal treatment under the law. In recent years, feminists have campaigned for rights such as good childcare, maternity leave and better contraception, as well as for freedom from violence and from sexual harassment.

FACT FILE

The United Nations takes action
The Fourth United Nations World Conference for Women, held in Beijing, China, in September 1995, was a landmark on the road to gender equality. All the issues that have come up in this book – and many more – were discussed by thousands of participants from all over the world. Human rights, economic independence and poverty, education and health, violence against women at home and in war zones, were all on the agenda. And, for the first time, gender was there, too. In the words of the *Platform for Action*, women and men have 'a mutual responsibility to achieve equality' – that is, things can only change if both women and men work together.

In some areas the gaps between women and men remain very wide, in others they have become much narrower.

As we have seen from this book, one reason why societies are changing is because women want a better and more equal world. Sometimes they have been inspired by feminist ideals. More often they are fighting for basic rights. But gender equality cannot come from the actions of women alone. If we are to make the world fairer for everyone, then women and men will need to work together for change.

Women and men, girls and boys, must work together to make a better world.

GLOSSARY

Condom A method of contraception used by men.

Contraception Methods used to prevent a woman becoming pregnant, used by women or men, or both.

Convention A formal meeting that often leads to the signing of an agreement.

Discriminate To treat someone in a negative or unfair way, for example because of the person's gender, colour, ethnic group or way of life.

Elections When people vote for somebody to represent them, in parliament or on a local council.

Family planning Belief in, and methods used, to decide the number and spacing (i.e. years between them) of children.

Feminism The system of values or beliefs that says that women are equal to men and should be treated in a fair and equal way.

Feminist A person who believes in feminism.

Gender How females (women and girls) and males (men and boys) are treated by society, and how society expects them to behave.

Maternity/paternal leave Time off work (paid or unpaid) for a woman/ parents before, during and after the baby is born.

Migration Leaving your home, village or country to move elsewhere.

Oral contraceptive pills A method of contraception used by women.

Politicians Leaders or decision-makers. In most countries today they are elected.

Sexual harassment When a person (usually a woman) is treated badly (e.g. threats, violence) because of her or his gender.

Sterilization A method of contraception involving an operation, on a woman or a man, which means the person cannot have any more children.

Trade union A group of workers who join together to protect or extend their rights.

Urbanization People moving from the countryside to live in towns or cities.

Voluntary organization A group or company working to improve society rather than to make profits.

BOOKS AND TEACHING MATERIALS

Fiction

Anne Fine, *Flour Babies* (Puffin Books, 1994). Boys learn about babies. 11+
Robert Leeson, *Smart Girls* (Walker Books, 1993). Based on folk tales. 10+
Jane Leggett and Sue Libovitch (eds), *Solid Ground* (Unwin Hyman Collections). Writings by women. 11+
Chloë Rugbon, *Virtual Sexual Reality* (Bodley Head, 1994). Justine turns into Jake. 13+
Jane Ure, *Come Lucky April* (Mandarin, 1993). Two very different societies discover each other. 13+

Information books

Women in History series (Wayland, 1989–91).
Women Making History series (B.T. Batsford, 1991-92).
Women and Power (Dryad Press, 1988).

Background reading for teachers

Julia Cleves-Mosse *Half the World, Half a Chance* (Oxfam, 1993). Examines gender roles.
Women in Development (ODA). A free booklet.
Women: Still Something to Shout About Nikki van der Gaag (*New International* Issue 270, Aug. 1995).
Women and World Development series (Zed Books, 1993-5).

Materials for teachers

The Backbone of Development, (Birmingham Development Education Centre, 1994). A photopack.
The Equalizer I, Activity Ideas for Anti-Sexist Youth Work (Bread, Bristol, 1991).
Focus for Change: Class, Gender and Race Inequality and the Media in an International Context by Sally Meachim, Dave Richards and Olukemi Williams (Focus for Change, 1992).
Shoulder to Shoulder (SEAD, 1992). A teaching pack.
Speaking for Ourselves, Listening to Others, Living in the City from a Gender Perspective (Leeds Development Education Centre, 1995). Main focus is on Nairobi, Kenya.
Women Hold up Half the Sky (CAFOD/Christian Aid, 1986).

Games

Encounters by Janie Whyld (Whyld Publishing Co-op, Moorland House, Kelsey Rd, Caistor, Lincs LN7 6SF, 1990). An interactive computer game.
Manomiya (Returned Volunteers Association, 1 Amwell St, London EC1R 1VL, 1984). A simulation game about African women farmers.
Who is she? (London Union of Youth Clubs, Girl's Fund, 64 Camberwell Rd, London SE5 0EN, 1993). A board game.

Videos

Man Made Famine available from *New Internationalist*.
Savithri (Christian Aid, 1992). A twelve-year-old girl from India talking about her life. 15 mins.

USEFUL ORGANIZATIONS

Australia
Australian Council for Overseas Aid, Private Bag 3, Deakin, ACT 2601.

Community Aid Abroad, 156 George St, Fitzroy, Melbourne, Victoria 3065.

Human Rights and Equal Opportunities Commission, PO Box 5218, Sydney, NSW 2001.

Office of the Status of Women, Department of the Prime Minister and Cabinet, Locked Bag 14, Queen Victoria Terrace, Parkes, ACT 2600.

The Women's Bureau, GPO Box 9880, Canberra, ACT 2601.

Britain
Action Aid, Hamlyn House, Macdonald Rd, London N19 5PG.

Christian Aid, PO Box 100, London SE1 7RT.

Development Education Association, 6 Endsleigh St, London WC1H 0DS.

Equal Opportunities Commission, Overseas House, Quay St, Manchester M3 3HN.

New Internationalist, 55 Rectory Road, Oxford OX4 1BW

Overseas Development Administration (ODA), Eland House, Stag Place, London SW1E 5DH.

Oxfam, Supporter Services, 274 Banbury Rd, Oxford OX2 7DZ.

Scottish Education and Action for Development (SEAD), 23 Castle St, Edinburgh EH2 3DN.

War on Want, 37-39 Great Guildford St, London SE1 0ES.

Womankind Worldwide, 3 Albion Pl., Galena Rd., London W6 0LT.

Canada
Canadian Advisory Council on the Status of Women, 9th Floor, 110 O'Connor St, PO Box 1541, stn B, Ottawa, Ontario KIP 5R5.

National Action Committee on the Status of Women, 57 Mobile Drive, Toronto, Ontario M4A 1HS.

Oxfam Canada, 251 Laurier Ave West, Ottawa, Ontario KIP 5J6.

New Zealand
CORSO PO Box 9716, Wellington.

Human Rights Commission, PO Box 5045, Lambton Quay, 8th Floor, Vogel Building, Aitken St, Thorndon, Wellington.

Ministry of Women's Affairs, 48 Mulgrave St, Box 10049, Wellington.

Oxfam New Zealand, Room 101, La Ganda House, 203 Kaiangohope Rd, Auckland.

Republic of Ireland
Department of Equality and Law Reform, 33-39 Mespil Road, Dublin 4.

Trocaire (Catholic Agency for World Development), 169 Booterstown Ave, Blackrock, Co. Dublin.

USA
International Women's Tribune Centre, 777 United Nations Plaza, New York, NY 10017.

Oxfam America, 115 Broadway, Boston MA 02116.

UN Development Fund for Women (UNIFEM), 304 East 45th St, 1106 New York, NY 10017.

National Organization of Women, 1000 16th St, Ste 700, Washington, DC 20036.

INDEX

Numbers in bold indicate subjects shown in pictures.